Behavioral Psychology

Research into mental processes and behavioral patterns is known as psychology.

JOHN BASU

Contents

Dive into the study of human development and change across the lifespan in developmental

HUMAN PSYCHOLOGY

A person's mental and behavioral processes are at the center of human psychology. Biology, psychodynamics, behaviorism, cognition, and humanism are some of the many schools of thought that have contributed to the field of research.

According to research on human nature, there are essentially four distinct personality types: optimistic, pessimistic, confident, and envious. These species represent 90% of the population.

The field of psychology is essential in helping individuals lead more fulfilling lives. People can better understand themselves and those around them if they take the time to study the fundamentals of behavior and mind.

Human psychology:

Emotional intelligence can be defined as one's ability to recognize and make sense of one's own emotions and those of others.
The concept of "emotional intelligence" (EI), originally proposed by psychologists John Mayer and Peter Salovey, gained attention when author Daniel Goleman popularized it. "Emotional intelligence" refers to a person's ability to understand and manage their

own emotions as well as those of the people around them.

- **Important characteristics of emotional intelligence include things like:**

Being self-aware is being aware of one's own mental and emotional state, one's own strengths and weaknesses, and how all of these factors influence one's behavior .

Being able to control your emotions in every situation is an important skill for emotional self-regulation. The ability to control emotions and quickly adapt to new circumstances are prerequisites for remaining calm under pressure.

Emotionally mature people are characterized by a focus on the future and the ability to recover from setbacks. When you hold yourself to high standards, you force yourself to grow and change.

Empathy is the ability to identify and understand the emotional state of another person. Being emotionally attuned means responding to the experiences of others with kindness and understanding.

Ability to interact with others
The ability to get along with others is the cornerstone of emotional intelligence. Communication, teamwork, and the ability to make friends are valuable abilities.

- **Some of the many practical benefits of emotional intelligence include:**

Those who score higher on the EI scale are more likely to be natural relationship creators and keepers. They are naturally good at putting themselves in other people's shoes, which helps them defuse volatile situations and foster fruitful conversations.

The ability to inspire and motivate their team while maintaining their composure under duress is the mark of leaders with good emotional sense.

People who score higher on the EI scale tend to be more resilient and more self-controlled under pressure.

Improving your emotional intelligence can lead to better mental health, greater self-awareness, and overall happiness.

Because of their heightened awareness of how their words and body language impact those around them, people with high EI tend to be good communicators.

Conflicts are easier to resolve when people with high EI can get to the root of the underlying emotions.

Emotional intelligence is a lifelong skill that everyone can hone. A more fulfilling and fruitful life can be a person's destiny with constant efforts to increase their capacity for self-awareness, self-regulation, and social connection.

Cognitive biases:

Investigate how anchoring, the availability heuristic, and confirmation bias might distort judgment.

Cognitive biases are pervasive tendencies to refute or ignore information that would otherwise lead to more reasonable conclusions. Biases in our decisions and judgments do not necessarily come from a lack of objectivity or logic, but rather from the brain's attempt to simplify information processing. We can see cognitive biases in action in the following cases:

When we look for evidence that supports our pre-existing beliefs while ignoring or minimizing evidence that contradicts them, we engage in confirmation bias. This can potentially reinforce pre-existing biases or incorrect beliefs.

Speed of Service Heuristic biases can arise when easily accessible information, such as recent experiences or notable cases, is used. We tend to give more weight to easily accessible information in our memories.

Anchoring bias occurs when we give too much weight to the first information we see, no matter how unimportant or arbitrary it may be, and it can occur when we make judgments. We use this first piece of data as a springboard to create our next opinions.

Overconfidence bias occurs when an individual gives an exaggerated impression of their skills, knowledge or the validity of their opinions. Most of the time, people believe their own predictions and opinions more than they should.

"I knew it all along" bias, also known as hindsight bias, occurs when people falsely believe that something was predictable or planned after the fact.

When people seek out and consider data that supports their own beliefs while ignoring or minimizing evidence that contradicts them, it is called confirmation bias.

The propensity to give more weight to more recent information or events while giving less weight to older data is known as recency bias.

Maintaining an unnecessary strategy simply because additional resources have been invested in it is known as the sunk cost fallacy.

The "ripple effect" describes how people blindly follow the trends, ideas, or behaviors of their peers without questioning or evaluating their own quality.

A self-serving bias leads us to attribute our successes to our own skills and efforts and to attribute our misfortunes to external forces, such as unfortunate events or luck.

Neglecting to take cognitive biases into account can lead to erroneous judgment, poor decision-making and a distorted view of reality. Being aware of these biases could help individuals make more reasonable and unbiased decisions when they could have a significant impact. To better understand human nature and find ways to combat it, researchers in fields such as psychology, economics, and marketing study these biases.

Psychodynamic:

Learn about the many ideas of personality, including the Myers-Briggs perspectives, the Big Five, and psychodynamics.

The frameworks offered by different personality theories help us understand and explain an individual's patterns of thoughts, emotions, and behaviors . Here are three popular personal theoretical frameworks:

An extremely popular and widely researched framework for analyzing human behavior is the Big Five personality model.

In it, the "five factors" are proposed as the building blocks of a person's unique personality. A person's receptiveness to new information and ideas is indicative of their intellectual curiosity and willingness to take risks.

A person's method , responsibility and self-control are reflected in his level of consciousness. The propensity to seek and enjoy the presence of others is known as extroversion, a personality characteristic.

A person's agreeableness can be judged by their willingness to cooperate with others and by the empathy and interest they show toward those around them.

A person's emotional stability can be described by their level of neuroticism. Based on the beliefs of Carl Jung, the Myers-Briggs Type Indicator (MBTI) helps determine a person's personality type. It uses four polarities to classify individuals into sixteen distinct groups:

Extroversion, as opposed to introversion,

Nose (N) versus Sense (S) Key distinctions Crossing of thinking and feeling Examining the relationship between perception and judgment (J) For example, "INTJ" stands for Introvert, Intuitive, Thought and Judgment, one of sixteen possible permutations of the four preferences. Critics have pointed out that the MBTI tends to group people into inflexible personality types and that there is little evidence to support its claims about its usefulness for personal development or career guidance. Despite its popularity, the MBTI has been criticized for these issues.

The importance of the unconscious in the formation of personality is highly valued in the psychodynamic theory of Sigmund Freud. Essentially, it consists of three main elements:

The most primitive and lowest part of our mind is the instinctive and hedonistic Id.

The ego is the sensitive aspect of a person's intellect that separates their illogical desires from harsh realities.

Our superego, responsible for our moral and ethical decisions, adopts societal norms and acts as our conscience.

According to Freud, several psychosexual stages impact character development. These stages include oral, anal, phallic, latent and genital stages.

These theories draw on different schools of thought and rely on different levels of supporting data. The Myers-Briggs Type Indicator (MBTI) has been criticized for not having sufficient scientific basis, unlike the Big Five model which is widely used in contemporary psychology and has significant empirical evidence. Although psychodynamic theories form the basis of the field, they have evolved and transformed in light of new information.

The examination of personality and its effects on various aspects of human behavior and functioning could be better understood by becoming familiar with these theories. Take a look at attachment theory, which is based in psychology and states that a child's emotional and social development is influenced by the bonds formed with their primary caregivers during their childhood.

Ainsworth expanded on the work of psychologist John

Bowlby in proposing attachment theory, which considers the impact of a child's early attachments with primary caregivers on the child's development and behavior in the future . The consequences of the bonds formed between infants and their primary caregivers are the major subject of this theory.

- **The main concepts and components of attachment theory are:**

According to attachment theory, based on their interactions with primary caregivers, children develop one of several attachment styles. These attachment patterns shape a person's social interactions and emotional regulation abilities throughout their life. Here are the most typical forms of attachment: Those who are secure in their attachment style are able to maintain both strong personal relationships and reasonable independence. Their communication with others is simple and truthful. Fearful of being left behind, people with an anxious and preoccupied attachment style obsess over their relationships to an unhealthy degree. They cannot function without the affirmation and reassurance of others. Maintaining independence takes priority over establishing deep connections for people with an avoidant-dismissive attachment style. They might be awkward around new people and have difficulty expressing their emotions.

disorganized) attachment type combines anxious and avoidant traits. Due to past hurts, people of this type may want to get close while remaining cautious. During childhood, a person forms what are called "internal working models" – mental representations – of how relationships work. The mental models that people use to interpret and respond to their environments have a significant impact on their expectations about future relationships.

primary guardian gives the child a secure base from which to explore the world. Constant availability and attentiveness of a caregiver promotes a feeling of security and autonomy in children.

A popular method for assessing emotional bonding in infants is the "Strange Situation" experiment, created by Mary Ainsworth. Separation and reconnection of caregivers with infants in a controlled setting is the goal of this method.

The quality of your relationships as an adult can be influenced by the attachment patterns you established as a child. Insecure attachment patterns can lead to relationship problems, while secure attachment types are linked to more trusting partnerships.

A person's attachment style can be passed down from generation to generation. When parents face their own attachment issues, it is more likely that their children will develop secure attachment styles. On the other hand, if parents do not resolve their own attachment issues, insecure attachments may persist in their children.

The principles of attachment theory can be useful in psychotherapy and counseling. With the help of their therapists, patients can better understand their attachment styles and develop more adaptive ways of interacting with others.

According to attachment theory, a person's social skills,

emotional regulation abilities, and ability to form and maintain relationships are all shaped by their early life experiences. The importance of nurturing stable connections early in life cannot be overstated when it comes to ensuring long-term psychological well-being and social success.

Mental health problems:

You should educate yourself about mental health issues such as bipolar illness, schizophrenia, anxiety, depression, and anxiety.

Whatever the situation, here is a summary of some of the most common mental health problems, along with descriptions of symptoms, explanations of their origins, and treatment methods:

- **Clinical depression:**

Depressive symptoms include persistent sadness, lack of hope for a better future, lack of interest or pleasure in things that were once delicious, changes in eating and sleeping habits, extreme fatigue, difficulty concentration and even suicidal thoughts. The onset of depression can be caused by a wide variety of factors. Treatment options include talk therapy (cognitive behavioral therapy, psychodynamic therapy), antidepressants, dietary changes, physical activity, and social support.

- **Challenges caused by anxiety:**

Extreme nervousness, fear or apprehension, as well as physical symptoms such as restlessness, sweating, tremors and difficulty concentrating, are all indications of this disorder.

Root Causes: A person's genetic makeup, chemical imbalances in the brain, traumatic experiences, and stress from one's environment are all potential triggers for an anxiety disorder. People who suffer from anxiety and depression may find relief through medications, relaxation techniques, behavior and lifestyle changes, and antidepressants.

- **Mental illness:**

Some of the many symptoms of psychotic illnesses include cognitive impairment, social isolation, difficulty expressing emotions, hallucinations (false sensory sensations), and delusions (false beliefs).

Root reasons: It is believed that there are several levels of transmission, nervous system and environment that contribute to the development of schizophrenia. A combination of antipsychotic medications, talk therapy, family involvement, and other psychosocial interventions may be used to manage symptoms and improve functioning.

- **Emotional instability:**

Manic periods (high mood, increased vitality, impulsivity) interspersed with depressive episodes (low mood, lack of energy, thoughts of uselessness). Genetics, abnormalities in brain structure and function, and neurotransmitter imbalances are among the potential causes of bipolar illness. Mood stabilizers (lithium, anticonvulsants), support groups, and psychotherapy (cognitive behavioral therapy, family-centered therapy) are all good choices.

- **Relationship with Obsessive Compulsive Disorder (OCD):**

Classic symptoms include intrusive, repetitive thoughts (obsessions) and the subsequent desire to engage in ritualized mental or physical actions (compulsions) in order to relieve distress.

Root causes: Genetic and environmental factors play a role in the development of obsessive-compulsive disorder. Cognitive behavioral therapy and exposure and response prevention therapy are two examples of talking therapies; another alternative is medication, in particular selective serotonin reuptake inhibitors.

- **Regarding post-traumatic stress disorder (PTSD):**

Some of the symptoms include difficulty feeling emotions, excessive alertness, feeling sad, avoiding triggers, and flashbacks or nightmares that bring up painful memories.

Root causes: Stressful life events, such as witnessing or being a victim of violence, abuse or even a simple accident, can trigger post-traumatic stress disorder (PTSD).

Medications, such as antidepressants or anti-anxiety medications, or cognitive behavioral therapy (CBT), exposure therapy, or eye movement desensitization and reprocessing (EMDR) may be tried. Remember that mental health problems can manifest themselves in different ways and to different degrees in different people. Integrative techniques often include multiple treatments, medications, lifestyle changes, and social support. If you or a loved one are showing signs of a mental health problem, it is crucial to seek the advice of mental health professionals.

Social psychology:

Use your knowledge of social psychology to explore how being with other people and participating in group activities can influence your emotions, thoughts, and behavior .

A subfield of psychology, "social psychology" studies the impact of interpersonal relationships on an individual's mental health and activities. Look for how our relationships with others influence our emotions, attitudes, and actions. Some of the most important subfields of social psychology are:

When people act, think, and believe in accordance with the

norms of the group to which they belong, we say that they have conformed to them. The phenomenon is influenced both by normative influence (the desire to integrate) and by the informational effect (the conviction that one is right in one's group).

Following orders from above, whether or not they conflict with our values or principles, is the essence of obedience. Stanley Milgram's famous experiments demonstrated how command and control environments can easily lead individuals to behave in destructive ways.

In "group dynamics," scholars examine the relationships between various social groupings. This category includes group polarization , groupthink, and deindividualization, all of which worsen pre-existing group dynamics or cause cohesive groups to make poor decisions.

How people form their identities in relation to the groups to which they belong is the central question of the idea of social identity. It illustrates how a sense of community can improve self-esteem and influence the perceptions of in-group and non-group members.

Research on these themes aims to understand how social categorization can lead to prejudice, discrimination and stereotyping. Stereotypes are commonly held ideas about groups, while prejudice and discrimination are unfavorable feelings and thoughts about people.

How attitudes are cultivated and shaped By manipulating people's beliefs and actions in ways that cause cognitive dissonance. When it comes to people, things, or ideas, social psychologists are interested in the formation and evolution of attitudes.

The word "social influence" describes the complex set of ways in which individuals' social circles shape their own values, perspectives, and behaviors . Here we talk about some persuasive strategies which include scarcity, social proof, authority and reciprocity. Compliance and reciprocity refer to the tendency of individuals to comply with requests when they feel a sense of reciprocity or when the request aligns with societal norms or obligations.

One definition of "social norms" is the set of expected behaviors within a particular culture. Norms can be either descriptive, describing the behavior of the majority, or injunctive, dictating specific actions that individuals must take.

The interactions between people from different cultural backgrounds and the way in which one's own culture influences their social behaviors , beliefs and norms are at the center of cultural and intercultural psychology.

Individuals' behaviors are influenced by their environment and the relationships they have with others. There are ramifications in areas such as leadership studies, marketing, group dynamics, and social change efforts.

Anxiety and coping strategies:

Look at the different ways people deal with stress and think about how it impacts your body and mind.

What we call "stress" is actually the body and mind's response to external forces such as pressure and tension. Although some stress is adaptive and even inspiring, long-term or extreme stress can have detrimental effects on mental and physical health. Everyone experiences stress in their own way, but it is a normal part of life. A brief summary is as follows:

- **The effects of stress on the mind and body:**

Prolonged stress can cause or exacerbate a variety of mental health problems, including anxiety, depression, and post-traumatic stress disorder (PTSD). Cognitive abilities such as memory, attention and decision-making could be compromised.

Stress can lead to a host of physical health problems, including heart disease, reduced immunity, gastrointestinal disorders, sleep disorders, and the development of long-term illnesses like diabetes and hypertension.

- **Stress management methods and strategies:**

A key part of problem-focused coping strategies is acting quickly to eliminate or reduce the cause of stress. Examples include things like asking for help, managing time effectively, and solving problems.

emotion- focused coping mechanisms to manage the emotional upheaval that stress can cause. Some helpful techniques include practicing mindfulness, deep breathing, meditation, and engaging in activities that bring you joy.

Relationships with others, whether family, friends, or support groups, provide social support that can help lessen the impact of stress.

Both the mind and body benefit from regular physical activity. Research indicates that it improves mood, decreases stress, and increases endorphin production.

A better lifestyle, which includes a healthy diet, adequate sleep, and reducing or eliminating alcohol, nicotine, and caffeine, has been linked to better stress management.

Time management skills, including the ability to make a plan , set priorities, and break down large tasks into smaller, more manageable tasks, can help people feel more empowered in their daily lives .

By actively working to replace negative thoughts with more positive or reasonable ones, you can improve your sense of well-being and reduce your stress levels.

Psychotherapy known as cognitive behavioral therapy

(CBT) aims to help patients identify and change the ways of thinking and behaving that contribute to their worsening emotional and mental health problems.

Engaging in hobbies, artistic pursuits, and leisure activities can help reduce stress and recharge your batteries.

When you laugh or make someone laugh, your body releases the feel-good hormone endorphin , which in turn reduces stress.

When thinking about ways to cope, it is essential to keep in mind that what helps one person may not help another. Learning to use various stress reduction techniques and recognizing when they are no longer effective is crucial to maintaining mental and physical health. It is advisable to seek professional help, such as therapy or counseling, if stress is having a significant impact on life or becomes too difficult to manage alone.

Human development and change:

Dive into the study of human development and change across the lifespan in developmental psychology, covering issues such as child development, adolescence, and aging.

The study of human development through its different phases is at the heart of developmental psychology. This field examines changes at multiple levels, including physiological, psychological, social, and emotional. The following phases constitute developmental psychology: The term "
fetal developmental stage "

describes the period of time between the start of a pregnancy and the actual birth of the child. The field of prenatal biology encompasses studies of embryonic and fetal development , the influence of genetics and environment on fetal growth , and related topics.

This stage of development focuses on the years when a child is an infant or toddler. Topics covered include sensory and motor development, attachment to caregivers , language acquisition, and reaching social and cognitive milestones.

In middle childhood, a child attends elementary school. It involves developing your mind, making friends, accepting your own individuality, and expanding your knowledge base.

The transition from childhood to adulthood is known as adolescence. The physical changes brought on by puberty, the changes in the mind, growing up, forming relationships, and discovering one's purpose in life are all part of it.

At this stage of development, called "emerging adulthood,"

the "coming of age" process had been underway for some time. Personal choices about one's identity, career, and close relationships are all part of it.

There is a clear progression from childhood to maturity. Young adults' priorities include developing their careers and relationships. In middle age, you should focus on making a difference in the world, starting a family , and accepting your changing body. The difficulties associated with retirement, old age and unexpected health problems are all realities that older people must face.

The social, psychological and physiological changes that accompany aging are central to this stage of life. Dementia, aging, social support, memory loss and mental decline are all covered.

The following is a list of fundamental theories and concepts in developmental psychology.

The debate over the relative importance of genetic predisposition (nature) and environmental variables (nurture) in determining an individual's personality and development.

The sensorimotor, preoperational, concrete operational and formal operational stages are identified by Jean Piaget in his theory of cognitive development.

People go through stages of psychosocial development, as described in Erik Erikson's theory, and each stage is associated with its own set of psychological and social obstacles (such as uncertainty about one's identity or place in society , etc.).

The influence of early attachment relationships with caregivers on a child's psychological and social development was elucidated by John Bowlby and Mary Ainsworth in their theory known as attachment theory.

A hierarchy of moral systems, starting with preconventional, conventional, and finally postconventional, is proposed by Lawrence Kohlberg.

To ensure that all children grow up healthy and whole, it is important that educators, parents, and legislators are aware that humans are dynamic and adaptable.

Incentive and recognition programs

⁞

Learn how setting goals can boost motivation and how the brain's reward system affects the behavior you want to see more of.

As a species, we rely heavily on our reward systems and internal motivation to get things done and achieve our goals. All of these mental operations begin in the brain's complex networks of neurons and neurotransmitters. A brief summary is as follows:

- **Motor force:**

There is both internal motivation (motivated by things like happiness, satisfaction, and a sense of fulfillment) and extrinsic motivation (motivated by things like praise or rewards). Extrinsic motivators include factors such as monetary gain, social status, and public praise, which come from outside the individual.

The self-determination hypothesis emphasizes motivators such as knowing one's place in the world, being good at what one does, and having supportive social networks. People are more likely to take charge and strive to achieve their goals when they feel competent, part of a community, and in control of their own destiny.

From the most basic (food and water) to the most complex (realizing one's potential), Abraham Maslow prioritized human needs. Meeting basic needs is the first step to making higher-level demands motivating.

A goal that is well-defined, measurable, achievable, relevant, and time-bound is what the SMART framework calls an effective goal. Setting clear goals and then rewarding yourself for achieving those goals can be incredibly inspiring.

- **The reward system in the brain:**

The Reward System in the Brain and Dopamine Dopamine, a neurotransmitter, is secreted in the brain in response to pleasant events. As a reward neurotransmitter, dopamine reinforces driving by increasing its pleasure   .

Two key elements of the brain

circuitry for rewarding behaviors are the nucleus accumbens and the ventral tegmental area (VTA). The ventral tegmental area (VTA) sends a signal to the nucleus accumbens , which in turn releases dopamine, whenever an action or event is related to pleasure.

As a component of the brain's reward system, dopamine contributes to the development of addiction because behaviors or substances that trigger its release can become rewarding, leading to recurring use.

People experience an overjustification effect when they lose interest in doing things they would like to do for themselves. Turning a hobby into a full-time job is just one example.

A brain mechanism called "delay reduction" prioritizes immediate gratification over delayed gratification. This can make it difficult to prioritize your long-term happiness over your immediate desires and cause you to act impulsively.

A knowledge of incentive structures is fundamental in many fields, including health, education, business and psychology. In order to help clients become more motivated, achieve their goals, and thrive in a supportive environment, professionals must first understand what motivates people to act .

Positive psychology:

Dive into the field of "positive psychology" to learn more about the study of what makes individuals happy and healthy.

Positive psychology aims to explain and encourage a variety of positive elements of life, including well-being, happiness, strengths, and optimal functioning. Improving the well-being of individuals is at the heart of positive psychology, the aim of which is to do more than just alleviate mental illness. Here are some of the cornerstones of this academic discipline:

- **Good mood:**

Meaningful Happiness and Well-Being (SWB): Pleasant psychology seeks to improve people's lives by studying factors such as life satisfaction, pleasant emotions, and having a meaningful or purposeful existence.

Positivity, including feelings of joy, gratitude and hope, has been linked to greater resilience and better coping strategies when facing challenges.

- **Personal strengths and virtues:**

Some of the 24 traits highlighted by the Values in Action (VIA) categorization that help people perform at their best are inventiveness, curiosity, empathy, gratitude and tenacity.

An important principle of positive psychology is that, rather than focusing on improving one's flaws, one should work to strengthen one's strengths.

- **Factors influencing human resilience and economic growth:**

To be happy and feel like you belong somewhere, you need to work on your relationships and encourage others to do the same.

Participation and Flow: Improving your mood and self-esteem can be achieved by engaging in activities that induce a state of "flow": complete immersion and enjoyment.

When individuals pursue goals that are in alignment with their core principles and values, they lead meaningful and meaningful lives, which increases their happiness.

A combination of two practices – mindfulness and gratitude – can cultivate and intensify positive feelings. Applying positive psychology principles in schools and organizations has been found to lead to improvements in classroom atmosphere, employee morale, and

organizational effectiveness .

- **Realize the positivist theory:**

Increasingly, traditional therapeutic methods use interventions from positive psychology to improve mental health and well-being.

Positive educators have begun implementing positive psychology ideas into their lessons to help children with their mental health, social skills, and academic success.

Positive psychology is used in business and management to improve morale and productivity in the workplace.

When it comes to health behaviors , treatment adherence, and overall quality of life, patients with long-term illnesses may benefit from positive psychology-based therapies.

The core principles of positive psychology are appreciating and cultivating one's positive traits, surrounding oneself with positive influences, finding purpose in life, and participating in meaningful activities. By drawing attention to these aspects, positive psychology hopes to improve people's quality of life.

www.ingramcontent.com/pod-product-compliance
Lightning Source LLC
Chambersburg PA
CBHW051838250726
48659CB00005B/1904